10 ThINGS I LEARNED LIVING ON an ISLAND

JaSON BLaKe

Cover Designed by Damonza.com

Edited by Kathy Carter

Published by Laki Press in Lihue, Hawaii

ISBN number: 978-0-9977116-1-5

This book is dedicated to a disparate crowd.

First, this book is dedicated to my husband Philip. Thanks for taking the leap with me to Paradise. There's no one I'd have enjoyed learning with more.

Secondly, this book is dedicated to the island of Kauai and all of Hawaii. I feel so blessed to live here and thank you for taking care of us.

Thirdly, this book is dedicated to my parents Mary and Randy, plus my steps Steve and Karen. I also dedicate it to my grandparents Angie, Henry, Gladys and Joe. All of you helped raise me, gave me the gift of life and each of you helped me learn valuable things. (Since I may not write any more books, I had to get you all in here!) You are all loved and I'm so grateful for EVERYTHING!

Finally, 10 Things I Learned Living on an Island is dedicated to Pele and the other Hawaiian gods. If you exist and however you may, I'd much rather have you on my side than not. Please help us to be better stewards of these gorgeous islands and this precious planet.

DID YOU EVER see *Pleasantville*, a movie that starts in black and white and later turns to Technicolor? That is still my impression of Kaua'i. If you've never been there, it's a trip you have to take at least once in your life.

My husband, Philip, and I moved to Kaua'i in March of 2005. We were determined to build our lives in a place that represented inspiration and to escape the Chicago arctic winters and sweltering, humid summers. Our first vacation to the Garden Island a few years earlier had hooked us like a drug. Our lives would never be the same.

Kaua'i seems like Paradise. Her lush green mountains and golden-sand beaches attract romantics from around the world. Kaua'i has been featured in dozens of Hollywood films and is one of the top honeymoon vacation destinations in the world. It's quieter and less developed than Maui or O'ahu and is geographically the oldest of the Hawaiian Islands. The rain and sun combine with her rich, fertile soil to create landscapes worthy only of daydreams. Scientists argue about exactly how many microclimates are on the island. They range from cool, mountaintop swamp settings to Sahara-like sand dunes that spill into the ocean. And yet somehow the natural beauty is real.

The Hawaiian Islands are among the most remote population centers on Earth. Hawai'i is over two thousand miles from California and nearly four thousand miles from Japan. So although those of us on Kaua'i have many of the conveniences of modern life and are part of the "first world," we are missing some features that are common on the American mainland, like Target stores, office parks, expressways, and high-rises. Connected to the outside world through the media and tourism, we sometimes forget how far away and seemingly alone we really are, way out here in the middle of the Pacific, until we're hit with hurricane or tsunami warnings. Rough seas or a big storm can mean no milk at the grocery store for several days, or people stranded on the other side of the Hanalei Bridge, unable to make it back to their home or resort. Life is beautiful, simple, and sweet, but still somehow tenuous and vulnerable.

At the same time, for me there is an exuberance to living on an island. Almost everyone who lives here can't imagine living anywhere else in the world. Each time I go to the grocery store or stand in line at a coffee shop, I run into friends, acquaintances, coworkers, and even people I may not like. Families rush to enjoy the beach when the sun is out. In the evening, instead of rushing to a restaurant, watching TV, or going to the movies, locals can often be seen sitting in the garage with the door open, drinking a few beers and talking story. While there is still conflict and politics, generally people here care for each other, and we have unspoken agreements to mostly get along and watch out for each other. A civility remains that can't be taken for granted in other places, even on Oʻahu, which is the most populous island and home to Honolulu. On Kauaʻi, it's even considered rude to beep in traffic unless it's to avoid a collision.

Originally, upon moving here from the Second City, I tried to impose my mainland views and ways of doing things on the island culture. I did so with very poor results. "Why hasn't she returned my phone call yet? It's been over a day!" "What's wrong with that waiter? We've been sitting here ten minutes and he hasn't even asked us if we want a drink." Privately I wondered why others often chose to let multiple cars merge in front of them instead of just one, or better yet, none. "Why did the local lady give me the stink eye? I didn't do anything to her." I had much to learn about fitting into this community and living on this island.

Eventually I relaxed and started to let Kauaʻi and

the island culture teach me wisdom. Instead of incessantly trying to impose my will on the existing way of life, I started to appreciate and receive the gentle grace of Kaua'i. Piecing together work for the first few years left me with an erratic schedule and often an abundance of free time. I was invited to volunteer for a local nonprofit and thought, "Why not?" The thought of volunteering had never even crossed my mind when I was an upwardly mobile city dweller. As I stepped out to help in the community more, friendships started to blossom and doors I didn't know existed started to open. I noticed I felt better and happier if I stayed connected to the land and sea by reminding myself to take a walk up a mountain trail or lie on a beach at least a few minutes per week. I started to let island life teach me the quieter melody that played below the pop music noise in which I used to reside. I allowed myself and my body to settle down and take in life instead of trying to demand how life and the island should be.

Over time, I came to see life on this island as kind of a microcosm for life on Earth. On Kaua'i, a mix of people from different cultures, socioeconomic statuses, and backgrounds are trying to live together on a limited piece of habitable land, surrounded by a mostly hostile expanse. Kaua'i is in the middle of the rugged and unforgiving Pacific Ocean, and Ni'ihau, the only other island you can see from Kaua'i, is open only to native Hawaiians. Similarly, our planet is surrounded by the vastness of uninhabitable space. Earth is home to a mixture of people from different cultures, socio-economic statuses, religions, races, and backgrounds who are trying to live together. Was there a connection from which I could learn? Perhaps. Pieces started to fall into place.

Just like everyone on Earth, we islanders, whether we find ourselves here by happenstance or by decision, work toward a sustainable way of life—working together, paying the bills, and ideally leaving something of value for whoever comes next. That's really the same as life more broadly on Earth, but scaled down significantly. On Kaua'i, we have to find reasons to keep going and are occasionally lucky enough to experience moments of grace and connection. It's the same everywhere on Earth. We do the best we can, we make mistakes, and when the stars line up and we don't stand in our own way, at least a spark of our humanity awakens beyond the concerns of the everyday grind. That happens to me on this island. And it happens for everyone everywhere.

Kaua'i's gentle lessons to me have been many and frequent. I assume some greater intelligence dumbs them down to increase my chances of getting it. I'm not talking about deep philosophical constructions that are only for philosophers or physicists to debate. I'm talking about simple human truths that could be called common sense but which we so rarely seem to consider often enough, particularly in a world increasingly being run faster and faster by those who speak the loudest.

Remembering the lessons of living on an island helps me breathe a little easier, drive a little slower, smile a little more, and get through another day. Sometimes I even get to do a little good for someone around me. Perhaps the things I've learned may help you too.

As you read, imagine relaxing on a tropical beach on a warm, sunny day, perhaps with a loved one, taking the beauty in and letting go just a little. It's fine to order a Mai Tai and take a break to dip in the water when desired. Even if a vacation in Paradise isn't on this year's calendar, maybe what I've learned, or remembered, while living on an island may connect with you. Maybe your life can feel as manageable as a tiny little island you could circumnavigate in a couple of hours. Maybe other people will look more like your friends and less like strangers. Maybe your day won't seem as serious, even if there's a heavy swell coming your way. Maybe you'll get your own lesson that will lighten your load or the load of your loved ones. Maybe the world won't feel quite as big and overwhelming and messy. Maybe you'll remember how fun and beautiful even a bad day can be.

1
The Earth is an incredible place, and we need to enjoy it.

THE FIRST TIME I ever saw the full grandeur of the Napali Coast in a boat, I was struck speechless. So was everyone else on the boat. I've now been on a similar boat ride several times, and the same thing happens whether the crowd is five people or fifty.

The Napali Coast is a sixteen-mile stretch on the northwest side of the island that is not accessible by car. It extends from Polihale Beach on the west all the way to Ke'e Beach on the North Shore. Most of the coast is made up of cliffs that soar as high as four thousand feet and are covered with lush green vegetation. The cliffs rise dramatically right from the Pacific. This area of the island has often been used in films to represent an unspoiled, never-discovered example of a mystical location. It's been one of the stars of both *Jurassic Park* and *King Kong*. The crown jewel of the area is the magical Kalalau Valley, which has been lived in by ancient Polynesians, escaped to by occasional outlaws, and camped in au naturel by the young at heart. When my eighty-year-old grandmother flew over the coast in a helicopter, I remember her remarking as she got off the ride, "How can anyone doubt that there's an intelligence greater than man when you see something beyond the beauty that humans can create?"

* * *

Philip and I started vacationing on Kaua'i just after Christmas 2001. By gay standards, we were in the honeymoon stage. It had been years since I'd had a legitimate vacation, and we wanted to do something special. There were two great places on his dream list—Hawai'i and Egypt. Because of the timing, so quickly on the heels of 9/11, we chose Hawai'i.

To many working-class Americans, Hawai'i represents perhaps the most exotic, yet possibly attainable, travel destination. Philip had childhood memories of a lady from down the street, Mrs. Julia Kragle, coming over with her scrapbook to brag to his factory-working parents about her trip to Huh-WOY-uh (the North Central Pennsylvanian pronunciation of Hawai'i). Mrs. Julia Kragle anointed the islands "the most beautiful place on Earth." This memory stuck with Philip, and for him, our visit helped fulfill a fantasy. For me, Hawai'i was a chance to get away, to enjoy my new partner, and to just unplug from my stressful job and workaholic tendencies.

I purchased the first Hawai'i guidebook I found and read about the individual islands. My parents had flown to most of the islands in just a week, and that seemed like too much work for me at that time. I needed more rest and less movement. I wanted to experience one island. If we liked it, we could always come back to a different island another year or take the all-islands cruise eventually. After reading through the guidebook, I was attracted to Kaua'i. It sounded more remote, more small-town, more lush. A mouthy bank rep I worked with at the time insisted, "You should go to O'ahu and visit Honolulu. Kaua'i is only for romantics. There's nothing to do." That settled it for me: Kaua'i it would be.

We departed Chicago on an afternoon flight on December 26, 2001. I was hung over from drinking too much at a Christmas Day dinner we had attended. A blizzard was moving in, and the runways and planes were piling up snow and ice faster than they could be de-iced. Our flight took off shortly before other flights were cancelled. It seemed that we barely made it off the ground. I watched out the window as the shades of dull gray drifted out of sight. I fell asleep, tired from the booze, the rich food, and the lack of sleep the night before.

Our main flight went to O'ahu, and we arrived

too late at night to fly to Kauaʻi. There are no roads, bridges, or ferries that connect the islands, so we spent our first night in Waikiki. In the morning, we woke up and looked out the window at the beaches. It was nice, but we each privately wondered, "Is that all there is?" Diamond Head was gorgeous, but the skyscrapers, the traffic, the stores, the crowded beaches? I wondered whether we should have saved money on the airfare and just gone to Mexico or a nice beach in Florida or the Bahamas. Had we done that instead, I could have afforded a more luxurious hotel. I prayed I hadn't made an expensive mistake.

Later that day, after practicing patience in the chaos of the interisland airport terminal, we flew to Kauaʻi. As soon as we started to land, the scenery changed dramatically. This was our first full daytime view of Hawaiʻi, and we were not disappointed. Rather, we were starstruck. We rented a convertible for the drive to our bed and breakfast. I have never experienced any car ride as breathtaking as that late afternoon drive north through one of the most beautiful landscapes in the world. I didn't even believe it was real. Our reaction to the scenery was like a competition: "Look at that!" "Oh, my God!" "Look over there!" "Incredible!"

Our activities over the next few days—several long walks on a near-abandoned beach, a helicopter ride through the volcanic crater, and the incredible Napali Coast boat tour—left us glowing and our souls well nourished. The Earth is a beautiful place. I used to know that somewhere. In Chicago, I used to walk more often by the lake. When I lived in the Southwest, I used to go hiking or venture to more natural parks. How had I lost sight of this?

On the last day of the trip, we even went to an open house—just for fun, or so I said. Something was cooking internally.

Our subsequent visits and eventual move to the island represented a radical beginning of reconnecting with what an incredibly beautiful planet Earth is. That first year on Kaua'i, we committed to near-daily afternoon walks on the beach, taking in the ever-changing coastline, tides, and sunsets. We talked about our lives, our work struggles, our challenges, and more things than we had regularly before. Removing ourselves from the snow, concrete, and traffic of the big city was just what the doctor ordered. Our dates became hikes, as we explored new beaches and discovered trails to waterfalls off the tourist-beaten paths.

It was magic. We saw more rainbows and whales during that first year than either of us had seen in our entire lifetime. We became more grounded and more realistic. We grew happier and more connected as a couple. Our minds and lives slowed down, and we began to breathe lower in our bodies. All of this occurred because we allowed life and nature to start to reveal themselves to us. We began to use their rhythms to pace our lives rather than constantly overscheduling and pushing for results as we had in a big city. We began to appreciate the Earth seriously again and realize what an incredible source of renewal and inspiration nature can be.

I would love to report that we've kept every one of those habits and are still seeking out unexplored areas of the island each week. That would be untrue. We learned early that one great vacation doesn't mean we don't have to pay the bills or have a day-to-day life. But I do connect with nature more and take more small adventures than I ever did in the past. After a hard day's work, we are more likely to eat on the lanai so we can look at the mountain and to take a walk after dinner before reaching for a glass of wine or turning on the TV. And when I feel frazzled and fried, I know that spending a few minutes lying in the backyard or wading in the ocean can put life in perspective faster than any meditation technique, goal-setting strategy, or pill—many of which I have previously tried. This year, I've committed to starting my scuba certification as part of this process.

My body knew a lot of this before my intellect did. We human beings belong on Planet Earth. At a minimum, we are incredibly privileged to live here. It seems to me that we are almost part of the planet, or that we resonate with it the way a tuning fork can vibrate in harmony with an instrument. I can't articulate my feelings in this area perfectly, but I have learned that we must not take this glorious jewel of a planet for granted. We must let ourselves be constantly rejuvenated in her loving arms—our big and beautiful momma Mother Earth.

In over a decade since moving to this island, I've not once regretted any time I "wasted" walking barefoot in the grass, lying on the beach, or hiking a new trail. It's easy to forget how beautiful and awesome this planet is, and it takes effort to break out of our routines. My prayer, after getting the gift of living here, is that eventually no one will ever get so disconnected and caught up in day-to-day drudgery that he or she loses sight of what a honor it is to be here live on Earth. If it takes a rainbow and a tropical forest to remind you, so be it. Our visitor's bureau can help you make your plans. But I also know I could have learned the same lesson in Chicago if I had merely slowed down to take in more of it. May you enjoy Earth-living wherever you find yourself right now.

The Earth is a beautiful place, and we need to enjoy it.

2
We can't bury our trash forever.

AS YOU DRIVE west on Kaumuali'iHighway on Kaua'i, you eventually start to see glimpses of a canyon network on the *mauka* (inland) side of the road. Eventually you reach the town of Waimea. From here, a serpentine two-lane road starts up the mountain and leads into the heart of the Waimea Canyon and Kōke'e State Park as high as four thousand feet above. Below one can see a canyon as deep as three thousand feet, made up of crags and gorges and a mixture of brick-red clay earth and vegetation, as well as glimpses of waterfalls and the Waimea River, which helped to carve out the collapsed volcanic crater. While the Napali Coast may leave you speechless, Waimea Canyon would be better described as "breathtaking" in a grand way. Mark Twain christened it "the Grand Canyon of the Pacific." Apart from its smaller scale and the view of the ocean, you might mistake a picture of Waimea Canyon for its much grander Arizona cousin.

* * *

But even amid such grandeur, a tiny island can have its own challenges. Our gasoline costs about a dollar more than on the mainland. Milk can cost as much as eight dollars per gallon. We have famous traffic on our main two-lane road, and the triviality of our local politics is derided daily in letters to the editor of our local paper, *The Garden Island.*

Beyond these petty nuisances, Kaua'i has at least one dirty secret that most people don't know about, one that unfortunately is shared by much of the developed world. If you drive past the road that goes up the mountain to Waimea Canyon and continue further west, far beyond where most tourists venture, you'll find a landfill that is overflowing. This is a problem that has been festering for about a decade.

Many of the other issues affecting the island are the subject of public debate: Where should we place a much-needed drug treatment facility? Should we have a barking dog ordinance, and can it be successfully implemented? How much development is too much, and where should it be? Should we cap the number of visitors to the island? We even have a debate over GMO crop production and pesticide experimentation that continues to make the national press. The landfill issue, however, seems more "out of sight, out of mind."

I got to visit the landfill once on a tour about recycling on the island. The trash and evidence of its burial goes on for hundreds of acres. But our landfill is nearing its capacity. We are running out of space for our own garbage. Currently, our landfill holds an average of one ton of trash per resident. Just imagine.

To be fair, Kaua'i, like many places, has initiatives to fight this ever-growing formation of trash. We have an above-average number of citizens who recycle by choice, and we have a "Zero Waste Kaua'i" initiative aimed at reducing our "diversion" by 70 percent over time. Progress is slow, however, and each win seems offset by the opening of a new store promising better goods, resulting in more items shipped to our tiny island and more packaging that will require disposal.

Many municipalities in America and around the world face similar or worse challenges, all related to how much garbage we bury, ship away, burn, or dump in some fashion. In many instances, as much as 90 percent of this trash is plastic that will not officially decay. My goal here isn't to start a debate that is beyond my nonexistent scientific credentials. But many people don't know even simple facts about our consumption. For instance, floating in the Pacific Ocean is the Great American Garbage Patch, or Pacific Trash Vortex, estimated to be at least as big as the state of Texas. One recent study says that by 2050 the oceans will contain more plastic than fish. Beyond that, we have carbon emissions that can't be buried either. When 97 percent of scientists and even the Pope weigh in on climate change and global warming, the problems of our consumption and waste have gone beyond fringe or tree-hugging movements.

On Kaua'i, the general consensus is that we need a new landfill site, and several have been proposed. At the same time, there's little talk of working actively toward less consumption, nor have we solved the ever-present American problem of NIMBY (Not in My Back Yard). Would we consume as much if forced to deal with our own trash personally? I know I'm amazed by how much our small household takes to the recycling station every week or two, despite our best efforts at reduction. Trash seems to be a worldwide problem that we generally like to ignore.

It's easy to forget about problems like these, which sometimes go unnoticed by the media, until one sees them up close and personal. Even then, the problems can seem insurmountable, too complex, or even too mundane, so our human inclination is often to just push them away. But how long can we continue to do this with our trash and with the environment?

For some reason, lately I've become much more aware of how much stuff our household of two adults and two dogs consumes. I'm not sure if that's a function of aging, or if walking each bag to the dumpster and driving the bins to the recycling station each week has put the issue more on my mind. We have an economy that thrives on consumerism, and doing our part to move the economy forward sure leaves behind a lot of packaging. I'm not really suggesting a solution other than paying attention.

On the island, "Reduce, reuse, recycle" is more a way of life than just a slogan or song. Our small-town radio station designates one morning per week when people can call in and sell or buy used items—farm equipment, tires, old vehicles, even office furniture. Often you hear, "It's free to the first person who picks it up." Having limited storage space, Philip and I have gotten into the habit of at least once a year going through all our closets and taking the household items or clothing we don't need to the local thrift shop. When the trees bear fruit, it's common for people to share their personal mother lodes of papayas, lemons, mangos, avocados, and more just to keep them from falling to the ground and creating a pig problem. Living on a tiny island, one learns to juggle and balance competing ideas, recognizing that both can be true at the same time—ideas like "There's only so much to go around" and "There's plenty for everyone," or "We should save this because it might come in handy" and "We should give it to someone who needs it more than we do." When you see that your personal choices do have an impact and make a difference, both positively and negatively, you start to pay attention just a little more.

Most of us have been hoping someone else would come clean up the world. A friend of mine jokingly and pithily reminds me, "Jesus is coming. Act busy." I don't know about you, but I kind of realize that sweeping world change probably isn't coming from some messiah or politician or mobile app. A better, brighter world is only gonna happen if more of us take a little more care in doing our part. If more of us aspire and work toward a planet that works and feels more like Paradise, we can enjoy it even more if and when that becomes a reality.

Even though Philip and I strive to keep up our home, it can turn into a mess. Whenever company is coming, we make a mad dash to get the place in order. Yet somehow everything looks better by the time our guests arrive. We can do the same with our world, no matter how big a mess it's in. Let's just start cleaning it all up today, one piece of trash at a time. As we care for our homes and communities and world, maybe we'll also start to clean up some of the emotional and psychological trash we all carry. After all…

We can't bury our trash forever.

3
We were born to
sing and dance.

KING KAMEHAMEHA THE Great is among the most respected of Hawaiian royalty. He is famous for having unified the Hawaiian Islands. Hawaiian Princess Bernice Pauahi Bishop created the Kamehameha Schools trust to educate the people of Hawaiʻi and perpetuate the language and culture. Kamehameha Schools impacts more than 6,900 students directly and has community learning outreach that reaches another forty thousand people annually. Being selected to attend Kamehameha School on Oʻahu at its Kapalama Campus assures a student one of the most, if not the most, well-rounded and prestigious secondary educations in Hawaiʻi and is a great starting point for continued educational and adult success.

Each spring the school holds a gala event called the Kamehameha Song Contest. The tradition dates back to 1922. "The objectives of the song contest are to build up the repertoire of the best in Hawaiian music for the cultural heritage of any student who attends Kamehameha; to develop leadership, cooperation and good class spirit; and to give students the use of their singing voices and to give them pleasure in singing as a means of expression." It is broadcast on television and webcast worldwide. At the contest, high school students compete in a choral competition that is unmatched nationwide. The event is held at the Blaisdell Arena in Honolulu, the largest non-stadium arena in Hawai'i. It is a hot ticket event and always "sells out," though it is technically free to attend. Families are limited in the number of tickets they can receive. The influx of families, faculty, and local dignitaries doesn't leave much room for outside people to attend.

In 2011, I had the honor of attending the annual Kamehameha Song Contest on the island of O'ahu. My spouse Philip lucked into tickets by virtue of being a choral teacher and having friends with tickets who couldn't attend. It was a transcendent evening. If you've never been in a great stadium with hundreds of incredibly voiced and trained choral singers belting out their hearts to near-sacred music, it is an experience that opens your heart and changes your cells.

* * *

Our first year on Kaua'i, a local attorney helped me

with some legal work. One day he said something like, "One of the community boards on which I serve could use some fresh blood. Would you be willing to help?" In a big city like Chicago, boards of directors for non-profits and big business were well out of my socioeconomic or status league. I'd never imagined the chance to serve and network in that way. I felt flattered, grateful for his service, and indebted for his wise guidance and advice, so I said, "Of course." Little did I know where this addition to my life would lead.

After a few board meetings for the agency, now called Malama Pono Health Services, I invited my friend Jeff to join me on the board. We helped the agency wake up to an important reality: without a big infusion of money, they would be insolvent within weeks. This was due less to mismanagement and more to a delay in receiving grant payments from large funders.

I was too broke personally to contribute significantly to the organization at that time, so I noodled on how I might best help. Fate and a nudging intuition stepped in. One of the odd jobs I had picked up after arriving on the island was as a performer in the local dinner theater show *South Pacific*. My landlord also happened to be a pianist. A light bulb came on—"Eureka!" I could create a singing fundraiser—a makeshift cabaret to raise money for the foundering agency.

Our little show was like a modern-day revival of a Judy Garland and Mickey Rooney movie. We rented

Līhu'e Parish Hall, and I begged a few friends to perform, including a local real estate appraiser who also happened to be the grande dame of the local community theater. Our "Emile de Becque" from *South Pacific* was a voice professor at the community college, so I twisted his arm to perform. I convinced my landlord to help the cause by playing as our accompanist. His partner, a professional event planner, helped dress the stage and rehang the tattered, dusty theater curtains. We talked the show up and up and up—around town, in the paper, and on the local radio. We printed flyers, hung them in coffee shops, and passed them out to the concierges at the resorts.

Before our show began, many questions plagued me: Would anyone come to our show? Would they like it? Would we be any good as performers? Could we raise enough money to make a difference? I didn't know the answers to any of these questions, but I plowed ahead and followed the next steps that continued to present themselves. After a lot of hard work and great effort, grace picked up the slack, and miraculously it all came together.

That first night, people from all ends of the island came to see our show, *Kaua'i Sings*. In one night, we raised over four thousand dollars for Malama Pono Health Services—enough to keep the doors of the agency open for another month or so. During that time we hired a new executive director with an expertise in financial repair, and together we began to stabilize and expand the agency, its mission, and its financial books, one step at a time.

The show also had a personal benefit for me. As merely a mediocre singer, I had previously been too self-conscious to pursue any singing endeavors beyond community theater and theme parks. However, attached to the greater mission of helping others and the community, I allowed myself the indulgence of performing, and I became a far better singer along the way.

Kaua'i Sings has continued for years, raising over $250,000 for local nonprofits. But the people in the audience, many of them regulars, don't come for the charity. Instead, they come to hear people—their friends, professional colleagues, family members—sing from the heart. It seems everyone loves to see people go beyond their inhibitions and just sing out. And the audience's favorite songs are so often the ones they know the words to and can sing along with.

I once saw a Facebook post with one of my favorite quotes from one of my favorite authors, Kurt Vonnegut. I think it has relevance here. He said, "Go into the arts. I'm not kidding. The arts are not a way to make a living. They are a very human way of making life more bearable. Practicing an art, no matter how well or badly, is a way to make your soul grow, for heaven's sake. Sing in the shower. Dance to the radio.

Tell stories. Write a poem to a friend, even a lousy poem. Do it as well as you possibly can. You will get an enormous reward. You will have created something."

Dance, chant, and song are woven into the Hawaiian culture through the traditions of hula. In case you didn't know, the first dancers of hula were men—quite a shift from our Western mindsets. Children here commonly start dancing hula at an early age and lose any self-consciousness about expressing freely and joyfully with their whole bodies. One of our favorite date nights is to go to the Grand Hyatt in Po'ipū and watch toddlers through teens professionally perform hula. This island has so much song and dance happening every night that tourists and locals could go to a different musical event every night of the week all year long if they choose.

As far as the greater world is concerned, dancing and singing have evolved in interesting ways over the past couple of decades. Television has taken us from *American Idol* to *So You Think You Can Dance* and *The Voice. Glee* was an instant hit, making it cool to be in chorus. No longer do you hear the denigrations of "chorus geeks" or "band fags." The movie musical has come back in style. Major television networks are performing musicals live in America on national TV. Technologies such as iTunes, Pandora, DVRs, Spotify, Netflix, and smartphones have put all the singing and dancing in the world just a click away. Why do we love music, singing, and dancing so, and what's causing the incredible revival?

I can personally chart my life's happiness and success in direct proportion to how often I have remembered and been willing to sing for even for a few minutes a day. Scientists show that more of the brain is in use while singing, and an early voice teacher told me, "When tenors sing, angels listen." Norman Vincent Peale, in his famous book *The Power of Positive Thinking*, encourages the reader to sing a song of praise or thanksgiving every morning. I've done so at times, and this practice does at least make an attitudinal difference, even if it seems silly or sounds horrible. All those songs I learned at summer camp did have value, even though in elementary and middle school we mocked them mercilessly. It's much easier to make fun of "Kumbaya" or "I've Got the Joy, Joy, Joy, Joy" when you aren't singing them than when you are. I dare you to find a song from childhood, sing it every day, and track your happiness for a month.

Who really sings or dances enough in his or her life? Remember when the entire nation held its collective breath and watched as President Obama led a memorial service in a rousing rendition of "Amazing Grace"?

I wonder if life in modern times could ever start to mirror the spontaneous expression of song and dance displayed in a Gene Kelly musical, or at least come a step closer. I don't know, but it would certainly be more interesting if we lived that way. Flash mobs hold our attention for that reason. I bet even a little more whistling while we work would somehow move us in the right direction.

The local people of Hawai'i have a general reverence for music. I've seen seniors sitting at McDonald's become surrounded by a crowd when one of them pulls out a ukulele and starts to sing an old local favorite. If you have never heard a real Hawaiian *kumu hula* (teacher of hula) perform an *'oli* (traditional chant), you still have life left to experience.

When we sing and dance, we are connected to positive forces bigger than ourselves, however we may individually define them. We become more present. I dare you to sing or dance for any length of time and stay crabby or upset. It can't be done. Mystics tell us the right tones help us to vibrate "at higher frequencies." Maybe yes; maybe no. Either way, it feels great to sing or dance one's heart out, even if it is alone in the house, in the shower, or in the car with the windows rolled up while stuck in rush hour traffic.

I remember the Coca Cola commercial from the seventies: "I'd like to teach the world to sing in perfect harmony..." I dare you to get outside of yourself to sing and dance a little more. For years, I wouldn't sing in public, even though I'd been told I had a great voice. The collision of my self-consciousness and desire of positive attention was too powerful to allow anything noteworthy to come out. Only when life forced me to sing for something greater than myself did I find the freedom to let loose and have fun.

There's enough music for everyone. Don't miss your chance to sing or dance. Nobody has your voice or can get down quite as badly as you. Don't forget…

We were born to sing and dance.

4
Everyone needs a vacation.

WOULD YOU BELIEVE that the number one vacation destination for Hawai'i residents is Las Vegas? At first glance, that seems counterintuitive. One would think that because they live in one of the most sought-after vacation destinations in the world, people in Hawai'i might not travel anywhere, except perhaps to a different island to catch the surf. But that is not the case.

It is estimated that Hawaiians travel to Sin City at least three hundred thousand times per year. Package charters, including transportation and hotel, make the trip more affordable than some interisland airfare and cheaper than even great deals to California. Local people have a passion for gambling, and many downtown Vegas hotels cater to "local-style" eating, serving breakfasts with Hawaiian favorites like Spam or Portuguese sausage. Many Hawai'i high school reunions take place in Las Vegas. I guess even those living in Paradise need a break sometime.

When you ask people from Hawai'i what they like about Las Vegas, the answers are varied. "I like that the tour company takes you downtown in a limousine, and when you get there your bags are already in your room." "I like the sports betting." "I like the buffets." "I like the shows. I saw Donny and Marie last time!" "I like the shopping. We don't have shopping like that here." "I love staying in the hotel, and every day you come back and someone has made your bed. It's the closest I'll ever get to having a maid!" When you add up the responses, there's a thread: even people from Paradise want a change of scenery.

***

Burnout led me to visit Kaua'i for the very first time back in 2002. I had worked for nearly ten years straight in Chicago, even on the weekends. I had dreams and goals of performing more often and moving into the upper class financially, but somehow those plans never seemed to get accomplished, despite my hardest work and best efforts. Even when earnings were good, some setback always occurred—my business market shifted, a relationship ended, a lease ran out and I had to move. Something always happened to keep my dreams in the distance, and they seemed to be moving further away and becoming ever less realistic.

A close friend suggested I take a self-development

course that had led to some significant positive changes for her, particularly in the area of relationships. Befuddled by the professional trajectory of my life, I decided to give her suggestion a go. It was a nine-day course based on managing one's beliefs. On the second day, I began a guided exercise that involved the following prompt: "What would you like to change?" I don't remember the exact phrasing of my answer, but it was something to the effect of "Working harder and harder and never getting ahead." Gently and kindly, the facilitator helped me unravel the belief structure that had created the frustrating circumstances of my adult life. How had I used my own mind to create a work and financial life that felt more like a prison than an expression of purpose, much less of joy?

The work was dicey and emotional. I began to think I had made a mistake by signing up and wondered about leaving. All of my resistance was up in full force.

Finally, the exercises began to work. I got a glimpse of life beyond my own mental and belief matrix. In a moment of grace and temporary enlightenment, I had a flashback of myself as a young boy, so distant from my father and desperately working harder and harder to get approval from a man who was too busy trying to make ends meet to notice me fully. This weird psychological influence from a long dead past had been guiding a good portion of my life, and I'd had no idea until now. After all, I now had a healthier relationship with my father and this emotional reaction that was guiding my day-to-day life didn't reflect current reality. I needed to change my ideas about what was possible. I had to create space in my life for different outcomes and begin to act more from a spirit of exploration than from my hard and fast assumptions about "the way things are." To cement this realization, I decided to commit to a real vacation, something I had never really done in my life.

This new spirit of adventure was a springboard into a magnificently high year of my life—more travel time, higher earnings, and a greater sense of purpose. I worked more effectively and got my finances in order. My sales-based income grew, and for a while I felt immune to the normal buffeting forces of everyday life. We had the vacation of a lifetime that year on Kaua'i, and we were lovingly cemented as a couple. I started to embrace my life with more enthusiasm and vigor. This was the first page of a new chapter of my life that would eventually have the heading of "Living on an Island."

Had I thought through the relocation more and known in advance what we would face during the first few years on Kaua'i, I probably never would have moved. Naively, I had believed that life would suddenly become easier if we lived in Paradise. I imagined that challenges would seem more like rainbows, money would flow like waterfalls, and stress would disappear like footprints on the beach. In my fantasies, I sipped Mai Tais and made business calls from the pool all day long until I retired in my mid-forties, somehow independently wealthy. We'd live the eternal vacation lifestyle. In reality, my work disappeared with the Great Recession of 2008, and for a long while I pieced together odd jobs and other work that I hated in order to make ends meet. Clearly I had more to learn, and living on an island was going to help life continue to teach me.

The move to Hawai'i was difficult for my husband Philip in different ways. He was a believer in public education and immediately got a job in the Hawai'i public school system. This was not the right fit. After trying to negotiate through workplace politics that he was unused to, he ultimately decided to exit the public education system. He took a job at a private school that presented a wonderful teaching and learning environment, but with major tradeoffs—the pay was lower, the benefits were less, and the workload was heavier than ever before. We had been transformed from the comfortable middle class to the struggling working class. This happened to a lot of people in America over those years after 2008.

I felt like I was back in the struggle I'd tried to leave behind in Chicago. We tried to visit our families on the mainland at least once per year, but that seldom seemed like a vacation. We leaned on island truisms like "Kaua'i tests you" and "This island forces you to see your true self, and you may not like it." Ultimate truth or not, those ideas kept us going through the rougher times.

During a desperate time for me income-wise, I posed this question to my inner guru on a yellow legal pad: "What can I do for work on this little island that could help us to survive?" The answer that returned made me recoil with horror at first: go sell timeshares.

"Oh, God!" I moaned. I was a major skeptic. My parents owned a lower-end timeshare unit in central Florida and were dissatisfied with the trades they had received over the years. I had miserable childhood memories of vacations in nearly abandoned resort towns during off-seasons, staying in musty condos where I slept on the thin mattresses of pullout sofa beds, trying not to tweak my back on the unyielding middle bar. I prayed silently that this wasn't what the yellow legal pad had in mind for my future.

To fuel my decision, I spoke to everyone I could find who sold timeshares in Hawai'i, from people who worked in high-end, brand-name resort companies to a lady who sold resale weeks of unknown condos from a dusty real estate office. The stories I started to hear contrasted with some of my preconceptions. I heard about sales representatives who sometimes earned solid income, and owners who were quite content with what they owned, vacationed every year, and made their vacations a priority.

My family had not really been enculturated with vacationing; we were too working class. Vacations weren't planned or expected. We did go on occasional trips, however. Almost annually for several years when I was a child, my grandparents drove me and my aunt (who was only four years older than me) to visit Disney World, which I adored. My dad took us to Panama City a few times and once to Nassau after a big year. Other travel was limited to the aforementioned timeshare trips with my mom and stepdad and all-too-frequent camping trips—all of which seemed, to a bookish, closeted gay, pubescent preteen boy, more like punishment than legitimate real vacations. No one in my family really thought of vacationing as an integral part of family connection time, rejuvenation, exploration, and adventure, and certainly no one ever asked me where I wanted to go or what I wanted to do.

When I started selling timeshares in Hawai'i, I realized my vacation DNA was definitely missing some chromosomes compared to the affluent crowd I started to meet—those who always planned at least one vacation lasting a week or more every year, and sometimes several. This was not a fact of life for me, with my working-class roots, or really anyone whom I had ever been around. I was intrigued.

Vacations are the often the first things on the financial chopping block when times get tough in America. Most Europeans, even lower-wage workers, expect their six weeks of vacation per year. In the United States, the rat race of getting ahead, the emphasis on consumerism, and increasing costs of living create financial standards and goals that we work toward tirelessly, sometimes to a fault. As such, the renewal of the spirit and the adventure of life outside the box can become secondary priorities at best, fantasies to be discarded at worst.

Selling timeshares, I was able to meet with hundreds of individuals, a broad spectrum of humanity, mostly from the United States. I met people at both ends of the vacation priority spectrum: the wealthy who vacation several months each year, and the struggling families with children who might get a vacation every four to five years. However, these polar opposites are not the norms. Most of the people that I met on a daily basis were average folks who vacationed somewhat regularly. That was an attractive way of life to me, and these people generally seemed happier.

Most US citizens long to see the wider world, to connect more with their loved ones, and to rejuvenate their inner spirits. Yet somehow most of us don't make these longings a priority, and our cultural institutions pressure us to ignore them. To most of us, frequent or regular vacations seem almost like a fantasy, something we'll attend to in retirement if we can. After the fact, I can attest that I may have been the worst timeshare sales rep in history, but encouraging others to plan and commit to vacationing at least inspired me to do so myself.

I was a workaholic in Chicago and moved to Kaua'i for a sweeter life. The timeshare sales work made me a vacation evangelist, yet I still managed to fall back into my workaholic tendencies. I had to consciously practice scheduling time to recharge, both on Kaua'i and by exploring the greater world. Even now, I haven't totally mastered the art of vacationing. The job did force me daily to really contemplate the value of vacations for myself, for my marriage, and as a way of nurturing exploration, adventure, and rejuvenation, even though I already lived on an island in one of the greatest vacation spots in the world.

Can a tourist ever be bored or depressed? Of course, the answer to this question is yes. I would postulate, though, that those emotions must be less statistically accessible when navigating as a tourist as opposed to in one's daily routine. William James, the father of modern American psychology, is reported to have said, "Every man who possibly can should force himself to a holiday of a full month in a year, whether he feels like taking it or not."

Philip and I started to vacation more, but it wasn't always easy to make happen. Our travels started simply when money was tight: a night or two on the other side of the island, watching a friend's bed and breakfast or checking into a Priceline.com hotel. Then, as finances loosened up, we expanded—five nights in Honolulu, a long weekend in Maui. We eventually secured our positions as Kaua'i locals by taking an extended Labor Day vacation in Las Vegas. We added Christmas in New York after a banner year, and recently we even spent two weeks in Tuscany. This year we are planning on visiting the UK. Other trips have happened and others are on the table. Often my eyes are larger than my bank account, so if our initial plans turn out to be too costly, we pare back to something more affordable, which can make finding the perfect deal part of the adventure. More staycations are in sight, too.

Many times, on the first day of a tropical getaway, I force myself to the pool. I make myself lie on a beach chair to relax. It isn't always natural for me until I've had a cocktail or nap from fatigue. Even relaxing can take practice. A shift of perspective, though, and passing time eventually conspire to allow me to breathe, and a new expansion begins, new space is available where none had existed. Relaxation leads to invigorated exploring that lets me decompress even more. I soon reach an elevated state where I want to see new things, taste new dishes, reconnect with my spouse, and restore my creative energy for the next steps in my everyday life.

Regardless of circumstances, everyone can benefit from taking a vacation at least once a year, somehow, some way. It's one of my wishes for other people. My dream plan, which isn't yet practical and still requires negotiation with my spouse, is two big vacations per year: one to explore some exotic place, and one to just unwind, read books, and walk on beaches. In addition to the big vacations, a few weekenders might be fun—for exploring the big city, for visiting other islands, for remembering why I love this island too. Will I get there? Only time will tell. Will I keep the dream alive? Absolutely.

In a perfect world, everyone would get to visit his or her idea of Paradise at least once in a lifetime. The bottom line is this: our souls can be free, even when our bodies, minds, and rents are not. As humans, we find ourselves mildly enslaved in so many ways—to our finances, to certain relationships, to political structures that work imperfectly, to medical conditions, to the media, to schedules set by employers, and even to technology. The list of taskmasters is diverse and real. Sometimes change can seem beyond reach, but the next step toward the destination is all we have to worry about.

Routines interrupted on purpose remind us that we are free in spirit. When one can taste that freedom and escape the necessary encumbrances of modern society, at least for a few minutes, the rewards are sweet indeed.

Not all vacations have to involve travel. If planning an actual trip seems like one more task on a never-ending to-do list, then smaller bites might be the right step. For me, a couple pages of journaling with my morning coffee is a type of vacation. A catnap right after lunch is a vacation. A walk around the neighborhood when I'm feeling dug in to work is a vacation. We can escape from daily pressures a little here and there.

A vacation helps me get a new perspective and a fresh start. Sometimes this means getting back on the same road with greater conviction, and other times it means being inspired to take a new turn in the road. Either way, we come back fresher and more alive.

What's the next vacation you can take? Remember...

Everyone needs a vacation.

5

We are not in charge, but we can make a big difference.

HAWAI'I IS KNOWN as a spiritual place. Many people are drawn to the islands for reasons they can or cannot articulate. This spiritual interest manifests in myriad ways. The many ancient temples, or *heiau*, that have been unearthed are visited by both tourists and people who revere Hawaiian and Polynesian cultures. There are an abundance of Christian churches, particularly those that were built by missionaries, from Seventh Day Adventists to Mormons. There are ashrams where disciples can study with gurus. There are Hindu and Buddhist temples. Most children here are given hula instruction, which includes not only dance and chants but also the sacred knowledge and hierarchies of instruction. There are an abundance of yoga teachers, yoga schools, retreats, and healing centers. And many people who live here, while not particularly devoted to any particular faith or teaching, consider themselves spiritual seekers or explorers of consciousness on some level.

It is said that before the ancient Polynesians immigrated to Hawai'i, Kaua'i was populated by the Menehune, an ancient, mystical race of little people who were master builders. According to legends, the Menehune were forest dwellers, shied away from other humans, and worked only at night. Two large, prehistoric construction projects on the island are credited to the Menehune—the Menehune Fish Ponds and the Menehune Ditch, both of which point to technology not available to other humans at the time and both of which would had to have been constructed by little people. Not unlike the leprechauns in Ireland, the Menehune supposedly exist in hiding today and are often blamed for things that happen in the night or mischievous changes that occur. If you can't find your car keys on Kaua'i, you'd better ask the Menehune what they did with them....

* * *

When I moved here, I probably would have reluctantly included myself in the spiritual or even "New Age" group, although I would have eschewed those particular labels because I did not want to be categorized. Many people like me either visit Hawai'i regularly or live here. Most of them have read many of the same books over the past thirty years—from those by authors like Louise Hay and Wayne Dyer to

A Course in Miracles and more. The idea that we can create our personal realities is exciting, and living in a place like Hawai'i that is gorgeous and happy and distant provides a wonderful experiment for that type of life exploration.

Before I moved to the island, for many years I had helped teach a self-development course that I mentioned in Chapter 4. Like the book *The Secret* and others, this course was based on the idea that we can more consciously create our reality. In alignment with this belief system, I read *The Secret* as soon as it was published. I wouldn't be giving due credit if I didn't say that this course and the work that I did through that milieu led to the idea, inspiration, and follow-through for my partner and I to follow our dreams and move to Kaua'i.

If you look back historically, the concept that we each create our own reality is a relatively new idea in modern consciousness. It seems that it started to plant itself in the human psyche beginning in the 1960s and grew and bloomed from there. That's really a short window of time when you consider that Christianity is over two thousand years old and Hinduism dates back over four thousand years. Many people argue that pieces of this idea of creating our personal realities were contained in all of those ancient religions in one fashion or another. But it was never really stated so succinctly until very recently on the human timeline.

From a spiritual thought perspective, that means it's pretty untested.

New Age writings were not the only places this idea cropped up in popular culture. It entered society in a big way with the making of *The Matrix*. At the same time, America saw the rise of the Christian "prosperity preachers," the movie *What the Bleep Do We Know!?*, and a decade with the highest sales of self-help books ever. Large group awareness trainings like est (Erhard Seminars Training, which eventually evolved into Landmark Education) and the seminars of self-help guru Tony Robbins soared in popularity over the past few decades, fueled by people who wanted to see what was really possible and how individually powerful they could be.

What I discovered with all my exploration was that, yes, we indeed create more of our personal reality, at least through perception, than most of us are willing to acknowledge. We do this both consciously and subconsciously. However, even if we are willing to take responsibility for our own reality, we all have blind spots—self-deception and subconscious influences that can muck up even the perfect plan for creating a dream life or big project.

What I came to realize through trial and error, though, was a very pragmatic thought that has been around since the beginning of time: things don't always turn out the way we imagine. You buy a dream house, but the market crashes. You produce your play, but the audience is not large enough to support the run. You meet the perfect potential mate, but he or she just isn't that into you. The universe has many competing forces that can push or pull, support or squash, our intentions through no fault of our own. We have to acknowledge these forces, even as humanity stretches together toward creating a more harmonious world for us all.

The other truth that is not acknowledged by the "we create our own reality" belief is that many wonderful things happen to us that we have nothing to do with, at least consciously. For me, these include my grandmother—who she is and her presence in my life; the way I met my spouse; and two different careers that I've adored and that compensated me very well, in industries that found me when I really wasn't looking. Personally, I've come to believe that some of the biggest disasters in my life were my own bright ideas, while the best things in my life have all come by way of grace, whether or not I quite understand what that means and how it works. Some of those wonderful things in my life—even the path that brought me to live on this precious island—involved circumstances and coincidences that happened somehow magically and easily, for which I'd feel foolish and arrogant to take any kind of personal credit.

I once jokingly said to my friends, "Why do so many people on this island—including me—talk about manifesting abundance, and yet we can't always pay the rent?" I knew this crowd and long belonged to it—the crowd who struggled to survive in the world while speaking supposed spiritual truths. People in this group of the great "ungrounded" sometimes had gifts that could out-shine people who had followed the straight and nar-row of more conventional life paths. They felt con-nection with the universe and other people. They had compassion and charisma. They felt and were often deeply kind. And they did their best to have positive attitudes, even when things seemed dark or bleak. They were generous, sometimes to a fault.

I eventually realized that this idea—that we cre-ate our own reality—requires balance. We may be able to influence our reality, but in certain moments that reality may not even extend past our emotions to the tips of our noses. Plus we have to acknowl-edge the very big realities that are already in place—gravity and weather; other people and their actions; societal and global influences; the strange roles that money, politics, and energy play on the world stage; and myriad other moving parts that animate our world. The whole mix of this amazing planet and universe cannot be ignored as we stretch to improve our lives and create a little magic. Because if we do believe wholeheartedly that we individually create our own realities, that we are the sole masters of our destinies, then we end up with nothing but guilt and shame whenever things don't pan out quite as planned.

Things happen that are beyond our control. At the same time, we can influence what happens in our life and our communities and sometimes the world at large. Do we each create our own reality? Or are there other forces—call them God, Nature, or fate—that dictate everything that happens, leaving us powerless to effect change? I think the real answer belongs somewhere in the middle of a sliding scale, and a large part of life is just figuring out where on the scale we fall today.

I believe in dreams. I also believe that sometimes they aren't meant to come true. It's inspiring to work toward fulfilling an aspiration or creating a better world in some way. At the same time, we must not take ourselves too seriously or think of ourselves as too important to the process. We are not in charge of everything. And that, I have come to realize, is ultimately a great thing.

In the movie *South Pacific,* which was filmed on Kaua'i, Bloody Mary sings in the song "Happy Talk": "You've got to have a dream. If you don't have a dream, how you gonna make a dream come true?"

If your dream does come true, awesome. If it

doesn't, well, that's okay too. Life might have something better in store for you.

We are not in charge, but we can make a big difference.

6

Your life is your greatest work of art.

ANAPEPE, ON THE west side of the island between Kalaheo and Eleʻele , is lovingly called "Kauaʻi's Biggest Little Town." The town's settlement predates the arrival of Captain Cook in 1778. Hanapepe is a bit of an anomaly because when you drive off the main highway into town, the architecture begins to look like you've entered a saloon town in the old American Wild West rather than a village on a tiny Pacific island. The mostly Asian immigrants who relocated to Kauaʻi to work on the railroads or at the sugar plantations included many skilled tradesmen like carpenters and architects. Many of these tradesmen had first worked in the American West and migrated here because of the opportunities. Their work influenced the architecture of many of our small towns, especially Hanapepe. Hanapepe's interesting looks have made it a star in many film and television productions, most notably *The Thornbirds*. Hanapepe's historic society has a great web page featuring more detail on the history and the wealth of community events available there.

* * *

Kaua'i, like many islands, is a magnet for artists. One of the favorite activities for tourists and locals alike is to drive to Hanapepe on a Friday night, grab a bite at a food truck, and stroll through the galleries, shops, and streets filled with artists selling their wares. Some of the galleries offer free wine and perhaps some light *pupus* (appetizers) along with the enticement of buying works of art priced from around ten dollars to tens of thousands. I believe that if you did a random survey of people who live on Kaua'i and other islands, you would find that the percentage who identify themselves as artists would be higher than the US average.

I believe that every human is an artist on some level and that we all have art to make. Some of us create the works that are traditionally labeled as art—pottery, paintings, sculpture, drawings. Others include themselves in the arts with dance, music, writing, acting, or some combination of these expressions. Art in all her manifestations is quite expansive. If you have ever seen a master salesperson from the sidelines, there is truth to the phrase "the art of the deal." The way some mothers care for their children or decorate their homes astounds me and shows the fluidity, organization, and intelligence of every creative human being. Indeed, if you don't believe that art is a gift provided by some larger force to help us express ourselves and find sanity and meaning, I dare you to doodle with crayons for ten minutes and tell me you don't feel better. It's impossible.

Some people make art as a profession. Some make art to tell the truth, either personally or collectively. Some make art for fun. Some intend to bring beauty into the world. Some people are just compelled to create and have no conscious reason for their art. Some, like me, have learned to practice arts habitually as a form of self-therapy and self-care. The reasons don't really matter, but I generally believe the world is better because of all kinds of art, even bad art. After all, good art never comes without some bad art first.

Personally, my parents lovingly mocked my crooning as I mimicked Debbie Boone and Air Supply as a prepubescent alto. I knew even then that it wasn't pretty. But I had to sing. Among the first of the latchkey kids generation, I'd rush to an empty home, find my mom's records of Broadway shows, and sing along to "If I Were a Rich Man" or "Some Enchanted Evening." Years of practice and a little training later, I can belt out an occasional showstopper with barely a critic. Again, bad art practiced usually leads to good art.

Many people feel called to create on some level.

It may be a painting, the next great American novel, or even new crafty stencils around the ceiling in the spare bedroom. We are always creating something in the world—good, bad, or neutral. I believe in a world with more singing, dancing, poetry, novels, murals, and even mason jars filled with multicolored sand sculptures. Have we figured out all the possible uses for old egg cartons? I seriously doubt it.

In contemplating art, there is another modality that we can be prone to forget: how our individual lives fit into the larger, sometimes brilliant, sometimes insane tapestry of society on Earth that we are, at a minimum, helping to create. If you could look at your life from the outside, would you call it good or bad art? Does it aspire to greatness or kindness? Would you like the picture to be prettier? Imagine thinking of your life as your greatest masterpiece: The art of living. The art of your life.

Even with lots of practice and some professional training, I was still making a lot of "bad art" in my life when I moved to Kaua'i. There was still a lot of strife and discord in my relationship with my partner. By the most generous definitions, I had a wavering career. By the most critical viewpoint, it was completely undefined, with myriad ungrounded goals and unfocused attention. This combination naturally led to unstable finances and a fair amount of debt. And it didn't escape me that although I was living in Paradise,

I was now practically on the other side of the world from the people I grew up with and called my family. There were still wounds, distance, and disconnection festering with some of them.

The graceful, loving nudge of the universe got me singing again, creating the fundraiser I spoke about in Chapter 3, and helping to do some good in the world. But while I continued to improve in those ways, I still needed more practice in the art of my life. I was chronically mildly depressed and professionally unfulfilled. It was time to spend as much time and attention on official art in the world—singing—and focused on some of the bad "life" art, which had no appreciative audience at all, including me.

What does your life canvas look like? Is it a masterpiece? A uniquely inspired expression? Or is it a misspelled, angry scrawling of the plagiarized thoughts of others? Is the art of your life bland and monochromatic? Or is it quietly beautiful, but locked up in a dusty closet that no one ever sees?

How are your personal relationships? How is your day-to-day enjoyment of life? How are your finances? Are you kind and honest to strangers? To the people you profess to love or call friends? To people who believe differently or live on the other side of some fence from you?

I think most of us agree that the world can be amazing, but also incredibly insane. Depression is at epidemic levels worldwide. We have to begin—one brushstroke at a time, one vocal exercise at a time, one forgiven person or random act of kindness at a time, one paid bill, one reconnection—to make better art of our lives, both individually and collectively.

On an island, it is tough to run away from the simple truth of how good the art of your life is or isn't. That guy you promised you'd pay back last week and haven't—you run into him in the grocery store here. The anger, rage, frustration, or anxiety you may struggle with—on an island you can't run too far before you hit the ocean and are left to deal with the feeling. On an island, that person you bad-mouth happens to be the auntie of the girl you are bad-mouthing her to. On an island, your neighbors always hear you when you're arguing too loudly with your spouse. On an island, everyone knows if you are a shark, even if you smile like a dolphin.

We have reached such a level of profound connection in the world. We have instant access to people across the globe through technology, currencies, and economic systems that are dependent on each other. We have the ability to be anywhere within about a day and the ability to talk to people on the other side of the world immediately. In some ways, the walls have closed in. We can't get away from each other or ourselves anymore. Ultimately that is a good thing. All of our human life-art has value. And it often impacts the rest of the world, whether we mean it to or not. So one could make the argument that we must take greater care to be aware of our impact in this connected world than people did in the past.

So make some traditional art, if that interests you. If nothing else, it's good therapy. But also don't forget the art that is the big picture—you and your life and your relationships. Your smile. Your health. How you treat your family. Your contribution to your community and your world. Your peace of mind. Your solvency. Your generosity. Your helpful spirit. Your personal je ne sais quoi. Allow the Great Artist to take pride in wanting to sign its name to what you call you and your life. In this endeavor, I promise you'll have at least one proud fan—yourself. And never forget, sometimes great art only comes after tearing it down to the studs or throwing out your first attempt and starting on a clean canvas. That's okay and part of the process. There may be some creative destruction as the first step of your life's art.

Make a masterpiece that you and those around you can always admire and reflect on for centuries.

Your life is your greatest work of art.

7
There is no room for armchair quarterbacks.

T HE FIRST OF May is a big deal throughout
Hawaiʻi. On that day, every year since 1929,
Hawaiʻi has celebrated Lei Day. There's even a
famous song by Leonard Hawk that goes:

May Day is Lei Day in Hawaiʻi
Garlands of flowers everywhere
All of the colors in the rainbow
Maidens with blossoms in their hair
Flowers that mean we should be happy
Throwing aside a load of care
Oh, May Day is Lei Day in Hawaiʻi
May Day is happy days out there.

Most, if not all, of Hawaiʻis public and private
schools have a daylong May Day celebration that is
always centered around a performance by the students.

I've been fortunate to witness it at Island School on Kauaʻi, where Philip is a teacher.

May Day is a remarkable celebration. Most of the classes learn different Hawaiʻi songs centered around the year's theme, which might be based on a particular part of the island's history or on some type of native Hawaiian flora or fauna. Usually the school's *hālau* (hula school) performs, with different hula choreography for each song. A band made up of teachers and outside professionals provides additional music. People affiliated with the school and from the community come every year to partake in the celebration. After the show, everyone sits down and eats a big *lūʻau*. This traditional feast might feature a pig cooked for hours in an *imu* (underground pit), a cooking method called *kalua*.

Even more remarkable than the show itself is all that goes into making the day wonderful. Sometimes the script and music for the show are selected as much as a year ahead by select faculty members and Hawaiian advisors. Teachers and students start learning songs and choreography months in advance. Parents volunteer to make costumes. Volunteers and employees literally build a stage to do the show on. The art department and students usually paint a large backdrop congruent with the theme. The afternoon and evening of the event, teachers and volunteers from around the island bring flowers and greenery from their yards to decorate the stage so that no industrial-looking piece peeks through and spoils the illusion. Aunties work for weeks making leis from many kinds of flowers for May Day, as leis are given out in abundance to teachers, students, and guests alike. On Kaua'i, the mokihana flower is often featured.

From the script to the performances to crowd control, to cooking the *kalua* pig serving food, and helping to clean up, everyone at the school—students, faculty, and dozens of volunteers and supporters—has a unique and critical role to play in making each May Day a wonderful success. The event wouldn't be as special if any pieces were missing. And it always is perfect.

* * *

The first draft of this chapter was written exactly one month before the next May Day celebration. My spouse was already deep at work on what he and his students would have to do to make the day a success. Since it was April 1st, it was also April Fool's Day. Father Bill, of St. Michael and All Angel's Episcopal Church in the town of Lihu'e, Hawai'i, posted on Facebook: "A Prayer for April 1st. God grant me the foolishness to believe that I can change the world." After a little Internet searching, I discovered this quote is a spinoff of a longer and even more beautiful Franciscan benediction.

Though I am not a member of St. Michael's Church, they do really great work in the community.

The church is very supportive of the arts and has many thriving ministries, including a great program called "Fishes and Loaves" that gives out free food, including locally sourced produce, to low-income people every Wednesday. Father Bill is a favorite island personality and a great author. The church is lucky to have him but will continue to prosper even when he moves on. His April Fool's Facebook posting inspired the theme for this chapter.

When I started visiting Kaua'i, I found vivid proof of the need for people to work together. Residents were still talking about Hurricane Iniki, which had devastated the island over fifteen years earlier. Iniki destroyed over fourteen hundred homes on Kaua'i and damaged more than five thousand. If you look at the satellite maps from the days of the hurricane, the island wasn't even visible under the storm—that's how enormous it was. The recorded footage of the destruction is incredible: roofs blowing off, houses collapsing, people unable to walk forward in winds over one hundred miles per hour, whole areas of vegetation uprooted and missing... strange, bizarre, and deadly.

Even fifteen years later, there were still signs of the disaster. On my first visit, I took a wrong turn and ended up at a shopping center that had clearly been abandoned since the hurricane had destroyed it. Once on a guided tour, I pointed toward an abandoned ramshackle hotel right off the road and asked, "What is that?" The driver replied, "That's the Coco Palms Hotel. It was destroyed in Hurricane Iniki. It was where Elvis's *Blue Hawai'i* was filmed. It's been vacant ever since."

And yet in most ways, the island has recovered dramatically since Iniki. Homes were repaired. New homes were built. New restaurants and businesses sprouted. Plans are underway to revive the Coco Palms. Tourism numbers are at an all-time high. With few exceptions, if you visit Kaua'i today, you might never find out about the hurricane that devastated the island and its economy for years.

I was moved when I learned, through personal stories and an episode of the Discovery Channel's show *Destroyed in Seconds*, how everyone came together after the hurricane. Tourists, short-timers, and people with homes elsewhere generally evacuated as quickly as possible—a wise move, since water, food, electricity, and other necessities were scarce or unavailable. But many people were forced to stay on the island and find a way to survive. Barter systems thrived. Hotels let people sleep in their ballrooms. Neighbors helped each other rebuild their homes. Food and water were shared freely. This was the miracle of human spirit that arose from such a disaster.

Indeed, this kind of spirit seems to prevail after great emergencies. Look at the disasters that have occurred in the last couple of decades—Hurricane

Katrina; the Indonesian tsunami; major earthquakes in Haiti, Japan, and elsewhere; terrorist attacks around the world; and who knows what will come next. Generally, when there is a major catastrophe, the walls come down between us and we roll up our sleeves, cooperate, and help out. No one can really shirk his or her responsibility during an emergency and remain a welcomed part of any group.

So what happens the rest of the time? Can we work together without a disaster to motivate us?

Sometimes it seems that the answer is no. In America, our politics have become so polarized that they are close to a farce—an ongoing reality show that, unfortunately, impacts nearly the whole world in some way. Everyone is certain about who should behave differently, who isn't acting correctly, and who is just plain wrong, ignorant, a socialist, or a Nazi. Where do these petty ideas reside in times of crisis? There usually isn't time or space for them.

Fortunately, I've also learned that even without a crisis, many of us can come together to do good. I've been recruited to do a fair amount of volunteer work since living on Kaua'i. It's harder to hide here than in a big city. I've seen firsthand that with a little injection of energy and elbow grease, a core group of people can create a whole bunch of good for a worthy cause. Oftentimes I have found myself busier on this island than I ever was when living and working in Chicago. Doing business here—be it work or volunteering—is usually empowering and energizing. My partner Philip also finds himself working harder than he ever has before, but he loves it because he can see what good results his work yields. We have more than once said, "We moved to Paradise to enjoy the eternal vacation lifestyle, and now we are working harder than ever. And that's okay." In the senior community where I focus my work, I find myself saying, "I'm 50 percent paid insurance agent and 50 percent unpaid social worker," and that's true if you look at how my days often go. We haven't minded most of the extra work because these pursuits are things we enjoy; they are for a good cause, and we are able to see the positive impact they have on our communities and the island.

We have also seen some bad habits that happen even in Paradise. In our work with nonprofits, both of us have noticed that although many people show up to meetings and have a wealth of ideas, few people are doers—those who are willing to say "I'll do it," "I'll move the ball down the field," or "I'll make sure that next action step happens." In fact, it got so annoying that at a board meeting for one nonprofit organization, I exploded: "Listen, I'm declaring a moratorium on new ideas! We have at least a thousand great ideas and no one to do them! Please do not bring up another great idea unless you are willing to take responsibility for it as a leader and make sure it happens. If we could take even 10 percent of the great ideas we already have and make them come to fruition, this agency would have an endowment in the millions." Perhaps my speech wasn't quite that eloquent, and I might have included a few expletives, but that was the gist. I've since been forgiven by the couple of people I insulted.

When I shared the story with Philip over dinner, he cracked up. In his work, where everyone is supposed to pitch in, some people get good at creating "boundaries" and adopting a "not my job" attitude. Of course, sometimes healthy boundaries are appropriate. But my hunch is that often these people are hoping that someone else shows up to do the hard part.

Do you know the children's story about the little red hen? The hen asks the other animals, "Who wants to help plant the grain?" Silence. "Who wants to help harvest the grain?" Silence. "Who wants to help grind the grain into flour?" Silence. "Who wants to help knead and bake the bread?" Silence. "Who wants to help eat the bread?" CHEEP, CHEEP, CHEEP, CHEEP, CHEEP!!! Philip wants to write a Kaua'i version of this, since the island has a huge, free-roaming population of chickens and roosters.

My grandfather was a first generation American from Poland. He was a working- class man and very Catholic. He and my grandmother had eight children together. My mother was the oldest, and as a result, I was almost treated like the ninth child of my grandparents. Though I wasn't enamored with sports, watching them was a way that our large family connected. We often surrounded the television while watching the football or baseball game, riding the highs and lows of the game quite vocally. My grandfather could tolerate your rooting for a different team from him and even your delight in his team's demise, but he despised criticisms about what should have been done. If someone said, "Why didn't he pass to him—he was wide open!" or "Why did the coach put him up to bat first? He should have been fourth," my grandfather would yell out, "No armchair quarterbacks!" It offended his honest, hardworking values that someone not in the game would dare to criticize those who were in the fight and doing their best in the moment. After all, who were we to criticize?

I love and hate great new ideas. Pushing the boundaries, building on knowledge, new technology—these ideas are all important. However, the world has plenty of great ideas that no one ever seems to get around to. Without cohesion and implementation, great ideas just lead to discord and decline. The world needs great ideas that are tried and implemented until they succeed or fail. If one idea fails, we can start trying a new one. Slogans, plans, hash tags, and eureka moments do nothing in the real world unless they inspire someone to take operational responsibility for making the ideas happen.

In our world, which is now dominated by social

media, a new catchphrase has taken hold: slacktivist. Slacktivists post articles or rant online about issues, but when it comes down to it, they don't practice what they preach. They complain about politics, but don't vote. They post about a cause they believe in, but don't donate or volunteer. It's not cool to be a slacktivist.

Are you sitting on an idea that needs doing? Does someone else have a great idea and need your help to make it happen? It's easy to make a list of things "they"—whoever they are—should do in the world. What is more interesting, though, is to consider how we can start to make a difference on the things "they" will probably never get around to.

It's easy to wait on "them"—our bosses, our spouses, our kids, our politicians, or anyone else—to come in and take action to improve things. But what if "they" never come to save the day? If you believe in a savior, and if he shows up, I doubt his first statement will be, "You did too much." Instead, his message would probably be, "We still have work to do, and I need your help. Get busy."

On an island, we can't wait for the politicians. We can't wait for someone else, our bosses, the rest of the world, or whoever. It's plain to see here: if we don't do it, probably no one else will either. A small island and this small planet demand all, or at least most, hands on deck in some significant way. Working together. For good.

We could just keep sitting back, complaining and hoping things improve. But that doesn't sound like fun to me. It sounds instead like a recipe for low-level anxiety and ungrounded, semidelusional hope, instead of real action that can yield real results and real satisfaction.

There are great times for watching TV. There are great times for enjoying football and drinking beer. There are even great times for armchair quarterbacking, as analysis is a useful skill and can be a great teacher. We just can't spend so much time on these endeavors that we fail to do good for ourselves, for those we love, and for the world at large.

Gandhi called us out in a very clear way: "Be the change you wish to see in the world." Imagine if each of us was at least some *part* of the change we wish to see. If Gandhi knew my grandfather, he probably would have said…

There's no room for armchair quarterbacks.

8

Put your own oxygen mask on first and then help the person next to you.

NDREW DOUGHTY, THE author of Kaua'i's most popular guidebook, wrote, "Coming to Kaua'i and not taking a helicopter ride is like going to the Sistine Chapel and not looking up." Based on this advice alone, Philip and I booked a helicopter ride on our first trip to the island, though on paper it was beyond our travel budget.

More than seventy percent of Kaua'i is not easily accessible by foot or car. The main highway stretches like a horseshoe, stopping near the west and north gateways to the Napali Coast. Geologically, Kaua'i dates back about six million years. The oldest of the Hawaiian Islands, it was formed when the Pacific Plate—the tectonic plate that lies beneath the ocean— passed over the Hawai'i volcanic hotspot. The island was born from the Pacific basin like cake icing being squeezed from a tube. Eventually, the plate continued to shift, which accounts for why the islands get geologically younger as you move through the island chain, ending with the Big Island of Hawai'i, which still has an active lava flow from the same hotspot.

The center of Kaua'i has a couple of huge mountain peaks—Kawaikini and Mount Wai'ale'ale, both of which reach well over five thousand feet high. This central part of the island is one of the wettest spots on Earth. The rainfall has resulted in the incredible Alakai Swamp at the top of the mountains, as well as countless craters that have been carved out over the millennia, where hundreds of waterfalls flow nearly every day of the year. That helicopter ride allowed us to see not only Napali and Waimea Canyon from better vistas, but also countless other private areas we might not have found on our own, including the Menhune Fishponds; Kipu Ranch, which is featured in many movies; and the famous Tree Tunnel. We witnessed 360-degree rainbows and countless locations normally discovered only by a multihour hike or a raft ride to a hidden beach. The helicopter trip left us a little high for the rest of that vacation and beyond.

* * *

If you're a frequent air traveler, you've no doubt heard "Put your own oxygen mask on before helping the person next to you" so many times that you no longer pay attention to it. The practicality of this safety advice is self-evident upon examination. I came to believe, while living on an island, that it's also a great life philosophy.

Raised in a good Catholic family with missionary blood and a knack for good deeds, I believe in a spirit of service to others. Doing our best to help those around us can have its costs as well as its graces. I've known people whose health and self-esteem suffered because they were so busy helping others. I've known people whose careers or significant relationships fell apart because they were working too hard for others. I've known people who worked hard to help others their whole lives, believing somewhat magically that everything would work out if they were good, helpful people. Unfortunately, that's not always true. At one point in my life, I was so busy volunteering that my finances were a mess and my spouse was tired of hearing about whom I had helped.

The problem arises if we haven't learned or don't practice self-care. Our lives can fall apart while we are busy "saving the world." Whom does that really help? An orderly personal life, meaningful relationships, sound finances, and good health are foundations upon which greater service to other people and to humanity at large can be built. However, some people are quick to think that just taking care of oneself—putting one's own oxygen mask on first—is selfishness. It's a distinction that requires discernment, and I think it's an important one to make, since I am also advocating that we all step up a little more in the world.

I am not advocating abject egoistic selfishness, nor am I indicating that nothing should be done for the good or well-being of others. Indeed, we all live together, so the idea that we might never require help from each other is ridiculous and even insane. Lending a hand in some way can be one of the most fulfilling human experiences possible, if not the most fulfilling. What I am suggesting, though, is that taking care of oneself and one's responsibilities, including those as esoteric as personal dreams and goals, is just as important as helping other people in the world. Indeed, it seems to me that the balance between self-care and helping others is a dance we best learn through practice.

The Hawaiians often use the word *kuleana* in place of "responsibility." *Kuleana* is a great word because it not only indicates responsibility, but also means "territory." It seems to me that a lot of life is about figuring out what territory is ours to manage and tend like a garden and what part is none of our business. On an island where everyone is in close quarters, figuring out one's *kuleana* is especially important.

How do we best take care of our own needs while at the same time serving humanity and helping others? Is perfect balance between service and self-care achievable? Probably not. But like everything in nature, we can aspire toward it and hit the balance point more often than not. Or perhaps we just notice when we are off kilter and shift back in the other direction. We dance instead of falling.

As Americans, we witness this deep imbalance in our politics. We've had a coarsening of the discourse. Some believe the ends justify the means no matter how corrupt or dishonest those means may be. Hate, divisiveness and misinformation have become thriving industries. The loudest voices on the left and the right often put ideology above practicality and progress, failing to consider that democracy requires managing many disparate voices with competing desires and kuleanas. The long-term goal has to be taking care of ourselves, our families, our communities and our world. My personal belief is that a great world goal is to reach a point where we don't export our unique problems to other places in the name of "helping." I recently had an adult awakening when I realized that in a true and properly functioning democracy, no one should be one-hundred percent happy with outcomes because that means we aren't truly compromising and working together for the good of all.

There is an old saying that we don't hear as often now as we used to: "Charity begins at home." Imagine a society where everyone takes care of his or her own responsibilities—bills, relationships, behavior, advancement—and does so thoroughly and generously, while still offering a hand to those who need help or are less fortunate. That's a goal I work toward. On a tiny island, it's a challenge to practice and the results are hard to miss. Of course, the ability to confidently work that plan requires that we have faith in some bigger shared vision and the general benevolence of people and life, even when they temporarily disappoint us.

Most religions teach that some form of self-sacrifice or self-abnegation is required if one is to be of service. At the same time, media images tell us to look out for number one, to become bigger and better than those around us, and to build bigger houses behind bigger fences. Both of these ideologies are insane when practiced without finesse or nuance. The former leaves you with a depressed sense of self. The latter leaves you with no genuine friends and perhaps more things to own than you care to manage.

I really like the garden analogy. We each take care of our own little garden and occasionally help our neighbors out too. As the garden bears fruit, our plot gets a little bigger, we can take on a little more and help a few more people in the process. Perhaps we share some fruits and veggies with our friends so they don't spoil. We take care of ourselves and we start to help others, little by little, until we are all doing our part and contributing together.

I grew up in a rural community in Georgia. One of the things I'm grateful for is being a member of a 4-H club. In case you haven't heard of it, 4-H is a nationwide youth development program that was started by the Cooperative Extension System and the USDA. In many rural communities, 4-H is the only nonreligious organization with positive, community-based goals for youth. When I was in high school, 4-H certainly directed my attention toward activities that were much more meaningful that just watching more television or playing more video games. It also kept me out of the trouble I could have gotten into with my friends if I hadn't had any positive direction. To this day, I remember the 4-H pledge because it seems to hit the mark on being a decent human being without indoctrinating any weird belief system. It reads:

I pledge my head to clearer thinking, my heart to greater loyalty, and my hands to greater service for my club, my community, my country, and my world.

A note to the self-obsessed (which is one of my own inclinations): perfection isn't a realistic goal, so give it up. Sometimes we can say, "Well, as soon as everything in my life is all lined up, then I'll start helping others and doing a little more good in the world." That's just a lame excuse that always moves the starting line a little further down the road, just beyond today or tomorrow. As it has always been, the world is now in some interesting times. There's no time like the present to help a little more. If anything, doing good for others helps you forget your own challenges.

My friend Liz was on a flight from Honolulu to the mainland when the captain came on the intercom. He said that due to engine trouble, they would be turning around and heading back to Honolulu. This happened when they were hundreds of miles into the Pacific, far beyond any landing strip should the plane go down. She said the hour they spent returning to Hawai'i was the quietest flight she'd ever been on. She admitted that even after forty years of flying around the world, she'd never really paid attention to the demonstration of how to use the oxygen masks. Jokingly, she said that if the oxygen masks actually did drop, she was pretty sure she would have died. Liz chided me, "Make sure you listen. I do now!"

What a great world it would be if we always kept our metaphorical oxygen masks on when needed and continued to help others with theirs. Which area of your own life needs a little more TLC? Put your own oxygen mask on. Is everything pretty hunky dory in your community? How could you help someone else?

Put your own oxygen mask on and then help the person beside you.

9
We all have a job to do.

KAUAʻI IS HOME to three of the five botanic gardens that make up the National Tropical Botanical Gardens. As explained on their website, NTBG is "dedicated to preserving tropical plant diversity and stemming [the] tide of extinction" of tropical plants. Their "gardens and preserves are safe havens for at-risk species that otherwise might disappear forever."

Two of the gardens are in the south part of the island known as Poʻipū, sometimes called Kauaʻiʻs "hole in the sky," since most days of the year find Poʻipū warm and sunny. Philip and I have a soft spot for the luscious Allerton Garden, which stretches from a private beach in southernmost Poʻipū to the border of the inland McBryde Garden. The area that is now Allerton Garden had a cottage that originally belonged to Queen Emma. Eventually, this section of the valley was sold to Robert Allerton, the son of a wealthy Illinois family. Robert had a longtime "companion" named John Gregg. To make sure his estate carried on to John, Robert adopted him in 1959. It was a very different time. Together, the men traveled the world, bringing together a collection of indigenous and rare plants as well as a variety of sculpture and water features. They arranged Allerton Garden into many different outdoor "rooms" to create different experiences and a meditative and otherworldly enclave far from the madding crowd.

Further up the valley, McBryde Garden is home to the largest protected and endangered collection of Hawaiian flora in existence. In 2007, Philip and I rented out McBryde Garden for a day and hosted a commitment ceremony. We said "I do" in front of family and friends, many years before marriage equality had reached Hawai'i.

Magical and fascinating in completely different ways, Limahuli Garden and Preserve is located at the other end of the island, in the town of Hā'ena on the North Shore. Limahuli Garden is set up in the same way that ancient Hawaiians farmed the mountainous terrain, with complex terrace systems built of lava rock. The garden staff work tirelessly to preserve only plants indigenous to the site, since so much of that flora is extremely difficult to protect. The most beautiful invasive flower or stunning sapling that does not belong there is derided as a "weed" and quickly removed, the way most Americans would tear crabgrass or wild onions from their pristine lawns.

***

I don't know if I had never visited any botanical gardens

before coming to the island and wouldn't have imagined myself a fan. Little did I know what incredible venues would surround us, what amazing beauty they hold, and what valuable jobs each of the gardens performs.

***

Employment can be a really funny thing on a tiny island. Before the Great Recession, most people on Kaua'i made their money via either real estate or something related to tourism. Even when the local economy was strong, many of the segments commonly found in metropolitan areas were missing here. For example, a friend of ours in Chicago works in human resources. When she starts a job search, there are literally hundreds of companies in her city that could be a match. On a tiny island like Kaua'i, there might be five companies with needs for a position like that, and maybe one of those positions opens every ten to twenty years. That middle segment of an economy—working class and professional jobs in medium to large businesses—is really limited here. The problem is compounded by the changes that have occurred throughout the United States with middle class job availability. Mostly, the people on Kaua'i who are well off either brought their money from someplace else, made a lot of money in real estate in the good times, or have owned a successful business that has found its niche in the economy here. The bulk of our working class is primarily made up of school teachers, blue collar workers, some tourism employees, government workers, people who work in the few banks, and so on.

Many of the people on Kaua'i, I dare say, struggle or have struggled financially in some way. It is more expensive to live here than on the mainland. A starter home can easily cost over five hundred thousand dollars. A gallon of milk averages over five dollars, and that's when it's on sale. Gasoline is usually at least a dollar more per gallon than on the mainland. Kaua'i has the highest electricity rates in America. And yet the pay scale is generally the same as or less than most places on the mainland. Even doctors make less than in many places on the mainland. To survive here, residents need to already be well-off or get creative.

Many excited people vacation here. Some of them like the island and the culture so much that they decide to move here. But they don't always have a plan, or the plan they have doesn't work the way they intended. Many of them end up moving back to the mainland after a few years. The ones who make it past three or four years tend to stay. Paradise can sure seem hellish if you don't have a job or enough income and aren't quite sure how to make ends meet.

Work was an easier proposition for my husband Philip when we arrived. He was a long-term public school teacher with a great résumé. The public school system in Hawai'i readily made a place for him. Later, when he realized he didn't fit in that system, he found a good position at a local private school. However, after ten years of working there, he's just now reaching the salary level he had when we left Chicago.

Finding out how to keep my own oxygen mask on while contributing on Kaua'i was a longer, more winding path for me. I was a financial professional when I arrived on the island. I started out working from home for the same company that I had worked for on the mainland. When the economy changed, my job went away. I wasn't sure what to do and spent years trying to figure it out. I knew I was already established in the community, so I tried to find what role I was supposed to play. I pieced together odd jobs for several years. In 2010, I was able to start my own business, and after a couple of years we stabilized financially.

We have seen many of our friends here go through similar struggles and evolutions. Friends that at first seemed to have it all, making us slightly envious, have found themselves carrying larger mortgages and earning less income after the economic downturn. Not just on Kaua'i, but throughout the world, many people are still working to find their way in the new economic reality. The future leaves a lot of questions for the average working person.

During the midst of my personal career crisis, I found a great book about mission, career, and contribution. I worked my way through it over several months. There are many great books out there like this. I was amazed that after sorting through the emotions, the bills, the confusion, the anger, the possibilities, the job listings, and the lack of job listings, eventually I did come face to face with a place of mission within me. Who would have thought that after all this time, at forty-plus years old, I was starting to tune into why I was on the planet, assuming it wasn't a completely random event.

Over the last decade, many people have had some type of work-related struggle. With the rapid evolution of technology and a more global economy, we've learned that solid ground may not stay solid forever. Some people have lost their jobs, changed careers, and even lost their homes. Many working class people have received pay cuts, either literally or when factored against the rising cost of living. Emotionally, the years since 2008 have been quite a roller coaster ride for many people worldwide.

Beyond all the potential work and weather upheaval on a small island, what's really important becomes very clear: I have to find some way to take care of myself and my family. We need a place to live, food to eat. If there's money left over, I might want to start saving. If I get past all of that, I might think about the higher levels on Maslow's hierarchy of needs. If that never happens, at least I can enjoy the weather. When I lived in the big city of Chicago, these simple priorities weren't quite as clear to me as they are here and now on this tiny island. If we are lucky, we find a way to pay the bills. If we are luckier, we find some joy along the way—though often the second part of that equation isn't clear until we've given some-thing a go. In an ideal world, we find a way to both pay the bills and really enjoy it. That makes for a very pleasant life plan, at least until the terrain shifts, which it usually does eventually.

There is something different, possibly special or inspired, about those individuals who aren't just going through the motions—those who are doing their job, whatever it may be, from a more cosmic sense of purpose. These people struggle with the same mundane challenges as the rest of humanity, but rarely are they thrown in the same way when something bad or unexpected happens. They often have more energy, are less apologetic about their existence, and show a confidence in their way of going about things that is palpable. I read one book that referred to this state as finding "the sweet spot." I like that description. When feeling the sweet spot, I don't wonder as much whether I am wasting my life or whether life itself has meaning. I just kind of know what I have to do and get on with it. I work my garden, share the bounty, and enjoy the view when I can.

There is a tendency in our society to see someone on a mission and notice how attractive his or her energy and persona are. We say, "That person's got something special! I want that!" And then we run off and try to emulate that particular person. It rarely works. One person's path or career or sweet spot is very different from someone else's. You can try to copy someone else, but somehow it never works. We have to keep looking until we find our own sweet spot.

Finding the sweet spot illustrates the value of going inside, of finding purpose and then pursuing it whole-heartedly, one step at a time. It's often the only thing that can put the darker times in greater perspective as we look back from down the road. It's the value of having clarity; overcoming ennui, existentialism or depression; of knowing we are making some difference, no matter how small, and staying plugged into that extra little juice that makes life meaningful.

Do some people seem to have charmed lives? Is it easier for some than others? Of course. That doesn't mean your life can't take on more meaning, that you can't become more fulfilled, that you can't make a more significant difference, that you can't feel more charmed yourself. I'm not there all the time, but I have tasted it in enough moments to keep me coming back for seconds. I would dare say that it keeps me closer to sane than just giving up. We've all met people much more outwardly successful than we are who really aren't happy, no matter how much they have.

Can we encourage and support each other to find our sweet spots? Or is this only a private struggle that one takes on? Is there an idea or action that would move you toward your sweet spot? If not, that's okay. It may be that the idea is only now planted in your garden and will take a little while to grow. Some of us have to spend a few years on rocky soil before we recognize the sweet spot when we find it.

Hawai'i is blessed to have many native-born and imported remarkable spirits. One of them is Kumu Hina. (If you haven't heard of her, it might be worth a Google search and watching the incredible documentary about her life.) Kumu Hina would now be called transgendered in the world and her early story is full of the pain and abuse experienced still by most transgendered people in the world. However, as part of her journey, Hina became an expert in Hawaiian studies. During those studies, she found that māhū was the ancient Hawaiian word for how she identified. She states, "Māhū are valued and respected in traditional Hawaiian culture because their gender fluidity is seen as an asset; the ability to embrace both male and female qualities is thought to empower them as healers, teachers and caregivers." Additionally, her teachings emphasize that it was very important in ancient Hawaiian culture to find one's role for society. Society was highly-ordered and everyone had a definite role, a job to do. As people fulfilled their roles, there was more acceptance of their differences because others knew the person was contributing to the greater good. This also helped the individual with self-respect, because when you know you are fulfilling a vital role, you feel better about yourself. Kumu Hina finds her mission in spreading this knowledge in many ways—by teaching Hawaiian studies and guiding a *hālau*, in a project against all forms of bullying, and by sharing the aloha spirit with all with whom she comes in contact. She knows her role, she has a job, and she empowers others to seek and find theirs as well.

On an island you can always take an early afternoon walk on the beach or a short hike and reconnect with whatever is real for you. Though perhaps in a less romantic way, the same process works in the middle of a suburban neighborhood. It works wherever you are. Even New York City has parks and empty churches. Take your walk on the beach and remember who you really are and why you are here. If you're not sure, then get some therapy or write in a journal—try anything, and then try something else, but keep going for it until you find your place and mission. Then get busy loving your life day by day, to-do by to-do.

Once you find your place in life, it gets a lot easier to be a little kinder and a little more loving to those around you. Imagine what might happen in the world if millions of people developed that capacity. That's the island I want to live on, and I think most people want to live there with me too. In Hawai'i, it's part of what they call "aloha."

Whenever you feel a little lost or a little off center, take a deep breath and remember…

We all have a job to do.

10
We are all in it together.

IF YOU'VE NEVER attended a *lūʻau* in Hawaii, you may have no idea what it is. Or you may think of the Brady Bunch's family *lūʻau*, which was private and on the beach. Times have changed, but that doesn't mean that attending a *lūʻau* in Hawaiʻi should not be on your bucket list.

Commercial *lūʻaus* in Hawaiʻi are big business and great fun. From a hundred to a thousand people are usually in a custom setting, perhaps a tent, a private garden, or an open structure built expressly for that evening's festivities. The menu usually consists of all-you-can-drink Mai Tais and a buffet-style dinner that almost always includes certain foods—*kalua* pig, fresh fish, lomilomi salmon, sweet potatoes, rice, an assortment of desserts, and, of course, poi. The evening includes live Hawaiian music and dancing, and usually an emcee who guides the audience, explaining the performance in detail and often aspects of traditional

Hawaiian culture and language. Generally, there's a reminder: The ancient Hawaiians didn't just eat until they were full. They ate until they were tired.

The history of the *lū'au* is actually quite interesting. Hawaiian religion, based on Polynesian religion, once had a complex code of conduct called *kapu*, which identified many forbidden practices that were said to be spiritually impure. There were *kapu* for everything, from the way you made a hook to how you built a canoe. Additionally, it was generally forbidden for men and women to eat together, and certain foods were off-limits to commoners and women. King Kamehameha II ended the *kapu* system. To celebrate the new age, he threw a great celebration and feasted with women. Thus the *lū'au* was born and continues to evolve for all kinds of celebrations.

One special kind of *lū'au* is known as the "baby" or "birthday" *lū'au*. Held on the first birthday of a child, it's a huge event, since the family basically invites everyone they know. Often the celebration includes special themes and planned entertainment. People bring cards and a monetary gift for the "money box." When the custom began, infant mortality rates were so high that many children did not make it to their first birthday. If they did, the family took it as a good omen and planned a huge celebration of the child's life.

No matter what type of *lū'au* you attend, one

of the main rules is that everyone is considered and treated as '*ohana* , or family.

* * *

In no way is life on an island perfect. Many of the frustrations of life in the mainland exist here to some degree. Our island has traffic. Our island has messy local politics. Our island has lines at the grocery store and the gas station right when you need to go there. People gossip and "talk stink" about other people. Business relationships thrive or go south. Coworkers can be annoying, just like in other places. Children have too many activities, and families struggle to get this one to football practice and that one to her hula *halau*. The mean-spiritedness and divisiveness that can play out on social media can infect even our small newspaper's letters to the editor. Taxes and infrastructure building are always controversial. We have mental illness and homeless people. The list could go on and on. Plus, Hawai'i is often identified as having the highest cost of living in the United States.

Generally on this island, however, people are kinder. People also seem more forgiving and less likely to hold a grudge. Of course there are exceptions, but these small, simple ways of treating each other translate into a quality of life that is just as attractive to outsiders as the weather and physical beauty of Hawai'i. Why is this so? There are many factors. The strong influence of Japanese culture on Hawai'i can often inspire one to leave more unsaid, or at least to measure speech a little more than the average American. Much of our culture can be attributed to the aloha spirit, which is a real thing and practiced pretty seriously by anyone who spends a decent amount of time living here. I also believe that things are a little lighter because, in a certain sense, we feel more "stuck" with each other and realize that at the end of the day, we need to work on getting along.

When I lived on the mainland, I had a sense of unlimited space and unlimited people, especially when I lived in large cities. On this tiny island, there's only so far you can drive to get away from a conflict. If you have neighbors you hate and you move as far away from them as possible, you're going to be at most about an hour away and are probably still going to run into them at Walmart or the gym. I'm much more aware here that if I consider cutting someone out of my life over a conflict, I could also be cutting myself off from someone I need in the future. If I cut someone off in traffic, I may bump into them in a few minutes in the grocery store. There are a couple of service providers in town whose service might not be perfect, but if I decided to "take my business elsewhere," I'd have nowhere to go.

And there's always the threat of a potential hurricane or tsunami. Hurricane season comes every year. We are advised to have a disaster preparedness plan for each household, but most of us don't have everything perfectly prepared. Somehow in the back of my mind I know that burning a bridge with someone could mean one less person who might help me if I need a job, food, or even water during a crisis. That has a way of putting things in perspective.

Ultimately, these things are also true on a global scale, but rarely are we as conscious of them in the same way. When the whole world is considered, it can be easier to worry about our own interests above the collective interests. Some things require help from the whole world, though. Combatting climate change is going to have to be a worldwide effort. The conflicts in the Middle East have influences that come from throughout the world and cause ripples that spread over all continents. Our financial systems are deeply interconnected. America, like most of the world, is not energy independent, and most people are now aware of what a huge role energy plays in our international politics. More and more people are waking up to the fact that it's not okay to exploit entire nations or continents for natural resources or cheap labor just because it's easy and cost effective. I certainly don't want my generation, or Americans in the long run, to be considered sophisticated pilferers. No matter what we do, we can't really get away from each other. We are all in it together, and perhaps we'd better learn to get along and help each other out.

I'm not a major donor by any means, but at least once a year I try to take a check to our local food bank. Ideally, I'll also make at least one food donation during the year. I'd love to tell you that I've always been a major humanitarian and my conscience couldn't have it any other way. Honestly, the truth is closer to the fact that I'm not comfortable with what I've heard about how severe food insecurity is in the world, in America—the wealthiest nation in the world—and even in Hawai'i. I'm also aware of how dangerously close I came, during our lean years, to being one of the people who needed the services of our food bank. If I contribute, I'll at least have the peace of mind to know that if I ever find myself in that position again, or worse, the resource will be there.

I know a community therapist who works with a large child population, many of whom are products of abuse of some kind. Recently she happened to show me a skill sheet she uses with some kids. It has a little drawing for each skill. The list was so basic, with skills like sharing, making friends, listening, speaking respectfully, expressing emotion in healthy ways, and controlling impulses. I'm certainly not perfect at using these skills, and the worksheet made me chuckle at how many I could stand to practice a little more deliberately. I can say that living on an island has naturally made me practice these basic skills more often than I did previously. I don't think anyone living anywhere in the world is at risk of overpracticing these skills.

I know you may not live on an island. I hope you can visit, but you may never be able to or even want to. That's okay. I hope I can help export these skills globally, though. I'm not sure there's an economic market for the skills of getting along, but I know there's a human market for them. I know I can make more of these practices and give them away more freely too.

If a virus can spread around the world in a matter of days, I'm sure a little more cooperation and kindness can too. After all…

We are all in it together.

MAYBE IF I were a faster learner or better writer, this book would be called *100 Things I Learned Living on an Island*, but that might not be as enjoyable a read. The good news is that life is always ready to serve me up another dose of learning, probably to keep me humble.

Still a novice scuba diver, I went on a guided dive a couple of weeks before writing this. When I was about fifty feet below the surface, a voice inside me said, "I'd really like to panic right now." Another, calmer inner voice said, "That's the worst thing you could do right now." So I kept breathing, put my attention back on the dive master and the turtles, and started to enjoy myself again. On the boat ride back to shore, it seemed like the wind was asking, "Did you get the lesson?"

It's now been over thirteen years since we started vacationing on Kauaʻi. I've lived here longer than I have anywhere else as an adult, and I finally feel like I've earned the right to call the island "home." If I add up all the lessons, the ones from the past and the ones that keep coming, I ask somewhat in jest, "What degree program are these a part of?" And a quiet voice answers me, "Love. You were born to love and live, and yet somehow you forget. You get caught up in the day-to-day details of life, you get indoctrinated by those with a vision, you get stuck in the struggle to survive, and you forget the basics—live and love."

I'm definitely not there yet, and I'm more skeptical than ever of those who claim to be. But I do like the journey that I hope leads to that understanding for me and all of us. I wish I could tell you I know what your answers and lessons are, so I could perhaps save you some grief along the way. For better or worse, life seems to personalize the curriculum for each of us. All I can suggest is that you be open to your next step and your next lesson. If a tropical vacation is your next step, then go for it. If writing a book is your next step, then go for it. No matter what your next step is, I promise it will be worth the ride, at least eventually.

It's a great time to be alive on Planet Earth. Who knows where it will all lead? What I can say is this: I am honored to share the ride around the sun with each of you. I wish you love, aloha, fun, and friends. If you find yourself vacationing on Kaua'i, take that hike, take that helicopter ride, take that boat ride or scuba tour—whatever calls to you. I promise you, you'll never be disappointed by one more adventure.

About The Author

JASON BLAKE IS originally from Conyers, Georgia. He moved to the island of Kaua'i in 2001 from Chicago, Illinois. Jason has been published in trade publications, in various newspapers and in magazines. 10 Things I Learned Living on an Island is Jason's first book. Jason is also the founder of the long-running fundraiser "Kaua'i Sings." He lives in Puhi, Hawaii, with his spouse Philip and their dogs Lucky and Stella.

Made in the USA
Columbia, SC
27 December 2017